In the Sunroom with Raymond Carver

In the Sunroom
with Raymond Carver

Poems

*Especially for Chris —
wish you were still in
Charlotte but I know your
life there in Durham is rich.
Still, I miss you! Be well!
Fondly,
Dannye*

Dannye Romine Powell

Press 53
———◆———
Winston-Salem

Press 53, LLC
PO Box 30314
Winston-Salem, NC 27130

First Edition

Cover image, "Cosmos in the Storm," copyright © 2020 by Dawn Surrat. www.dawnsurrat.com
Used by permision of the artist.

Cover design by Kevin Morgan Watson

Author photo by Laurie Smithwick

Library of Congress Control Number
2020933025

Printed on acid-free paper
ISBN 978-1-950413-22-5

For Julie Gaillard Suk

Acknowledgments

Many thanks to the editors of the publications in which the following poems first appeared, some in slightly different form.

32 Poems: "Once We Had a Daughter" and "She's Missing"

Arts & Letters: "Dead" and "Someone You Once Knew"

The Atlanta Review: "The Moviegoer" and "I Am Trying to Deliver Something to You"

Baltimore Review: "Tourist Season" and "Early Autumn"

Beloit Poetry Journal: "I Woke Today Thinking of Chloe Robinson" and "Motel"

Birmingham Arts Journal: "Chains" and "The Secret"

Cold Mountain Review: "In the Night, the Wind in the Leaves"

The Hollins Critic: "While Cleaning Out Old Letters to Me from My Husband's Former Girlfriend"

Madness Muse Press Addiction/Recovery Anthology: "The Bag" and "After He Goes into Rehab"

Nine Mile: "Longing Remembers Visiting the Red Rocker Inn," "Longing Weeps at the Barbecue Shack in Cashiers, North Carolina," and "Longing Waits in the Narrow Garden"

North Carolina Literary Review: "Poem for an Old Miami Boyfriend" (as "Because I Won't Be There When He Dies")

Ploughshares: "When They Called to Say She Had Died"

Postcard Poems and Prose: "Grief"

storySouth: "Red Mower, Blue Sky"

The Southern Review: "For the Love of Clothes"

Tinderbox: "Why I Hate Matinees" and "What It Was about That First Marriage"

Grateful thanks also to those in my life who nurture, advise, listen and sometimes endure, above all my husband, Lew Powell, who, though not a poet, is a master grammarian and an abhorrer of excess, as well as my cherished fellow poets: Julie Funderburk, Judy Goldman, Lucinda Grey, Patricia Hooper, Susan Ludvigson, Katherine Soniat, Julie Suk, and Dede Wilson.

Contents

III.

I.

In the Sunroom with Raymond Carver

October.
Here in my bright sunroom, you,
Raymond Carver, grinning, your cap
and sweater like those
of the young boys
in "Happiness."
Here's the thing, Ray. May I
call you Ray? Alive, you were older
than I. Dead, however, you
are only fifty, and now,
unbelievably, I have
a son your age.
A son, I might add,
who drinks night and day.

I have a question.
(Sure, Ray, go ahead. Prop
your feet on the coffee table.
That's fine.) In your poem
about Christine,
you said, *Daughter,*
you can't drink. You said,
It will kill you. Like it did
your mother and me.
Did she listen, Ray? Did she stop?
Alcohol is killing my son, too.
He doesn't listen. He keeps right on.

So here's the real question:
How did you manage to grab
at happiness, Ray, even while Christine
drank her life away?

In "For Tess," you said
that at times you felt so happy
you had to quit fishing.
You said how you lay on the bank
with your eyes closed,
listening to the sound the water made,
and to the wind in the tops of the trees.

That's a lot of happy, Ray.
I want that, too. I'm older now
than you, and before I die, I want
to feel the wind in my hair.
I want to feel it down to the roots.
I want to wrap my arms
around the world and sing.
But the words get stuck in my throat,
Ray. They get stuck.
And all that comes out is his name.

The Bag

The sheriff from the next county calls to say
someone found our son's duffel bag
in the autumn woods. We meet the deputy—
all close-shaved sympathy and stiff beige—
at a shopping center near the county line.

He hands over the bag, bulging
with last summer's trouble.

I'd watched him pack
the shiny black thing: cigarettes, journal,
pens, his beloved vodka
wrapped in a shirt,
that stupid scented candle in a jar.

I'll be back tomorrow, he'd said.

Finally, the inevitable
call, the fan of airy promises. The lost
cell phone and broken glasses.

Now the bag rides on my lap, heavier
than a bag of dirt,
clumsier than a sack of bones.

The Son

A narrow road unravels
through yesterday's hill country
and again I'm wandering
the old farmhouse,
brown and brittle.
I climb the stairs—
familiar worn floors,
four bedrooms, each as square
as a cake pan, occupants
gone, barely a trace.
Except here, in this room,
where I open the door
to find my son motionless
on the bed, his face
to the wall.

Wait. This is not
my son. No. This boy
belongs to that woman
I keep passing
in the wide hall.
It's her son who won't
wake, her son so pale and still.
I watch as she shakes
and shakes him.
I am going to kneel with her
by his bed and wait.

Chains

For hours, heading home
in our '73 Ford, we'd skidded
and slid through a whistling winter storm,
our two-year-old son asleep
in the backseat.
Yes, we had chains
in the trunk but we were clueless
how to attach them, inept
as we were at so many things
back then—love, parenthood,
the tricky footpaths
of a marriage
that wouldn't hold.

But that night, after miles
of white-knuckled panic,
we pulled into the back driveway
of the Victorian house where we rented
three upstairs rooms,
and saw that the yellow porch light
had transformed
the frozen landscape
into burnished gold.
You turned off the engine
and we clung to each other, certain
we had made it home.

Longing Drives by the Old Apartment

where she lived
with her first husband
and two young sons, back when
she kneeled by the tub
to bathe the boys, then tucked them
into the big double bed
with the soft ridge down the middle.
She can see them still: their fat, rosy cheeks
and slicked-back hair, the blue flannel PJs
with the silver racing cars.

And sometimes as they slept,
She would tiptoe in and pry open
their small hands
to inhale the coppery mystery
of each palm. Is it even possible
she did this here,
upstairs in this building,
that from the street
looks so much the same?

Once We Had a Daughter

though she wasn't exactly
ours. We bathed her
and kissed her and rocked her
to sleep. Oh, she was
a keeper, that girl. One day, maybe
a Saturday or a Sunday,
we bought her a red balloon.
She sat in her stroller
and held it by the string,
our three faces open
to the sky. She let go
or maybe she held on
and we watched the balloon
float away and away
into the enormous blue.
Some days we try to remember.
You let go, I say. *No, you*, he says.
I remember. It was you.

I Woke Today Thinking
of Chloe Robinson

You once told me that Chloe Robinson
got it into her head
you wanted to marry her
and before you knew it, her mother
had selected Chloe's wedding dress
and all the bridesmaid dresses
and you had to quickly disabuse her
of that crazy notion. Soon after,
you married me. So why is it
some days I mistake myself
for Chloe Robinson though I have never
even seen her photo. There I'll be,
on a balmy afternoon, walking past
a store window and I'll turn
and say, *Hello, Chloe*, to my image
in the glass. And always
we are wearing a long white gown
and the most beautiful, translucent veil
billows out behind and the look
on our face—well, it's sad.

What It Was about That First Marriage

The floors were fine. Gorgeous,
in fact. Blond as sunshine, clean,
polished, alive with the kind of promise
we had dreamed. But oh, those two
mismatched tables. Same height,
so we kept trying to line them up
as if they were a unit. One was maple,
right out of somebody's 1950's Nebraska kitchen,
with a scalloped leaf that folded down,
though it was years before we saw it
for what it was. The other, streamlined,
sleek. Once, we tried pushing them together,
covering both with a patterned cloth,
though dinner guests kept banging their knees.
When I look back, I'm amazed
we didn't toss it, haul it to the curb.
But, no, we struggled for years
to make it work, painting,
painting again, turning it sideways.

For an Eight-Year-Old Grandson
Whose Parents Recently Separated

He believes
if we dig deep enough
where we are weeding
around the rose bushes,
we might unearth a path
that belonged to a farm family back
in the 1800s, a family that kept cows
in the barn and maybe a few chickens.
Dig deep enough, he says, and we might even find
the house where the mom scrambled eggs
every day while the dad sat with the news.
The whole family woke up dead
one morning, he tells me—mom, dad
and their boy—and maybe if we get real lucky,
if we dig really deep, we might find
the holes where the bullets went in.

The Secret

Light glazes the near-empty streets
as I drive. Beside me, my grown son asks
if a secret I thought I'd kept buried
is true. A secret
that can still catch fire.
We stop on red. A bird flies
by the windshield. My father's words:
Easier to stand on the ground
and tell the truth than climb a tree
and tell a lie. Now, I think. Tell him.
I stare at my son's profile,
straight nose, thick lashes.
I remember, at about his age,
how a family secret fell
into my lap, unbidden.
That secret still ransacks a past
I thought I knew, rearranging its bricks,
exposing rot and cracks,
changing the locks on trust.

Let's Imagine I'm Trying
to Deliver Something to You

Something in a manila envelope,
several sheets of benign-looking papers,
no surprises, no recriminations.

To reach you, I sometimes take the elevator,
sometimes the back stairs. Always
I am waylaid or the weather

interferes, wind whipping my legs,
making a nuisance of my skirt. Occasionally,
I mistake your door for another

or at the right door, the wrong person.
Yesterday, a plump woman
in a patterned apron. Once, as I approached,

your brass mail slot vanished. Maybe
you don't need these details. Maybe you don't
even need the manila envelope

with its sheaf of innocent paper.
All that matters is this flame,
this lunging flame of my intent.

The News Reaches Me

Stones waver in the shallows
of the Nantahala River,
a cathedral of trees
on the far bank.
A green morning
if there ever was.
A car screeches, teeters
on the edge
of the old bridge,
plunges into the water.
Sudden leaf shudder,
birds flung into the air,
all the wild darting and flapping.

Longing Remembers
the Red Rocker Inn

A place in the mountains
she and her husband visited years ago.
The woman who owned it
sat on the porch swing
and told them her son had died
at sixteen. Longing couldn't believe
how serene the woman seemed, how brave
and unscathed. Longing herself
was young then, still a brunette
and slim, her own son barely twenty
and already a drunk. Now he's made it
to forty, a miraculous feat,
though Longing's not making any bets
on the next ten. Sometimes
Longing wonders what happened
to the woman at the inn,
if she still spends evenings in the swing,
one narrow black slipper pushing against
the porch floor to keep herself going.

The Minister's Advice to Longing

It's embarrassing
to tell—her son who tries
but won't or can't
stop drinking.
He lives in a house
with no lights, reading
C.S. Lewis and Augusten Burroughs
by day, his wooden chair tilted
against the side porch,
doors and windows wide
to the elements.

Yet he's still alive,
says the minister.
All these years, you thought
any day you might find him
dead and here he is
still breathing. Let's suppose
there's no hope,
he says. Suppose
he never does get sober.
Go to him anyway.

Longing tries to imagine
driving out to his house
with bread and cheese,
maybe a bottle
or two of seltzer.

Somehow
all she can see
is the weedy path
to his door,
that beat-up lantern
in the kitchen window,
its flame flickering, flickering.

After He Goes into Rehab

for the fourteenth time, we drive to his white house in the grove
of stalwart oaks and we round up the empty vodka bottles and we
round up the empty rum bottles and we round up the empty MD
20/20 bottles. We check the lights and water, flush the toilet once,
twice, bag the dirty clothes, wipe down the filthy Fridge and sort and
stack the wrinkled bills because that's what we do when we say we
will never, ever do that again. And after a couple of weeks, a letter
arrives through our mail slot, arrives like bloody murder, and the
inky words look shaky and the promises look watery, and we forgive
him because that's one more thing we do when we say we will never
do that again.

For the Love of Clothes

I'm not sure I was sincere when I wrote
to my dead friend's husband this morning
that I felt nestled in his late wife's arms

as I sat propped in bed wearing
her beautiful periwinkle cardigan, the cardigan
he insisted I take yesterday when he invited

me over to go through her things.
The truth is I'm thrilled to call that sweater
my own. Also the broomstick skirt

of vibrant blues and greens, a skirt
my friend and I had both seen in a window
a few years back and she got the only one

in our size. Also her soft, pastel scarves,
and that two-piece silk with the sprays
of orange flowers she found in Paris.

I know it cost a fortune, and now
I have something perfect for summer
weddings. Not to mention the blue glass

earrings. I'm almost ashamed of the joy
that filters through me when I hold them
to the light. I have to wonder if

I would trade these gorgeous things—I forgot
the stunning blue wool poncho—for my friend
to be alive again? Of course I would.

But if you must know, I don't relish the idea
of her returning to rummage through my closet
for her heavenly blues—oh, she would do it so gently,

so graciously, that's who she was—then packing them
into her car. Would I try to hide the broomstick skirt?
Would she even miss the silver pin with the round blue stone?

Sometimes Longing Craves a New Wardrobe

Silk gloves to the elbow, gowns
the color of black grapes crushed
on the tongue and staining
the lips. Turkish skirts, a fragrance
from Ethiopia. You never know.

When Longing wearies—
and she always does—the fancy
trappings float to the floor.
Only now does she bow her head to unclasp
the moon's silver cord from her throat.

II.

Weight

I was a skinny kid, all bones,
so my grandfather, who owned
a lumber company and with it a scale
for weighing nails, would hoist me up
into its tin bucket once or twice
each summer visit to see if somehow I'd gained
a pound or two. My mother stood by—why
does memory scrawl worry over
her pretty face?—while the bucket swayed
and settled, with me standing upright,
and, finally, the long black needle
that landed on my weight. My grandfather
would boom out the number
as if declaring victory over a minor
principality. Odd that during these sessions
I could feel my mother giving up
all authority over me, her only daughter,
until we were nearly equals, almost pals,
her father, my grandfather, the man
in charge of the scale, of the sawing
of lumber out back, its pitched aroma
wafting indoors, of the heavy paint cans
lining the walls, of the tubs of nails
and screws, the concrete floor, the vaulted
wooden ceiling and now even of my own weight
as he lifted me down, big hands circling
my rib cage, his lit Tampa Nugget
nearly colliding with my cheek.

Why I Hate Matinees

It's that sharp divide, entering in the bright
lap of day, exiting in the dark, stars

jagged, the wind with its cold surprises.
It reminds me of the time

my father pulled me close, his arm
around my shoulder—a rarity—maybe

a first. Ninth grade and I couldn't wait
for school the next day. I planned to wear

the pink jumper I'd made in Home Ec.
I saw the warning on my mother's face

as she watched me soak him in.
I wanted to believe

his sudden embrace
was as true as the white flower

that bloomed on our rock wall
once every hundred years.

Now a wink, a squeeze. *Tell me,*
sweetheart, he said, a lopsided smile

at my upturned face,
where'd your mother hide my bottle?

Longing Weeps at the BBQ Shack
in Cashiers, North Carolina

She blames it on the music,
the guitarist over there
under the trees
belting out "Sunday Morning Coming Down,"
a song her son played
back in his teens. No wonder
her tears, last night's news
that he's hitting the bottle again
still salty and raw. After
all these years, Longing believes
she's grown accustomed
to this seesaw of slurred promises
and boozy refusals, believes
she can go through her days
without giving him much thought.
And usually she can—until the words
to the old songs drift by
and she remembers back to a time
when she kept his Legos
in the blue plastic tub, his toy soldiers
in the red one, and no matter his havoc,
she could pick up all the pieces
and make everything look just so.

We Took You In

Had we seen you stumble
up the front walk, promises
drifting from your pockets
like lottery tickets,
we would have merely cracked
the door, allowing in nothing
but air.

      Or so we like to believe.
Now you are gone again
and I imagine you somewhere
out there, propped
against a building,
your shadow long and lean,
or in the woods huddled deep
in your coat. It's always dark
where you are. It's always cold.
All night I watch the moon
try to follow you home.

She's Missing

She must be chasing the cat—
hem of her white linen dress
flying around the fence.
Her voice inside the wind,
its strings and high shellac.
She'll be back
any minute, dragging
that old doll
with the flimsy velvet hat.
Any minute, no matter
the stars collapsing
into their sea of black.

Someone You Once Knew

Never mind the DNR instructions
in her chart back at the nursing home,
she was resuscitated seconds ago.
Now she's propped on a gurney, white hair,
white sheet, the blank look
of her hazel eyes. She could be
a pale-faced stranger, maybe
an old neighbor, someone
whose name you can't recall.
She attempts a wave
and you recognize that narrow hand,
the blue tributaries
of those veins,
the small diamond on the gold band.
She's coming to, this tether,
your mother. You could grow deaf
watching the awful noise of her quiet face.

My Father Comes to Visit Today

I hear first his infernal wings
as he swoops in through the back door.
Next I smell the elements
he carries with him. Some indefinable odor
that always sets me on edge.
He starts right in: *Are you saving
as much as you spend? Doing anything
with those expensive ballet lessons
you took all those years? Dad, I'm sixty-one,*
I say. He starts dealing the cards, fluffing
those terrible wings. *I didn't want you,
he says. I thought you should know.*
I know, I say. It's OK. We stare
at each other across the table,
brown eyes locked. He lifts one wing
as if to shrug. I bite my lower lip,
shuffle the deck. We look down, draw
for the deal, only one of us ashamed.

When They Called
to Say She Had Died

She was old, my mother,
and dead now, or so they said,
and I could think of nothing
but boiling pots of water.

Out the window,
November's birds pecking
the dry grass.

More and more water
I boiled, watching it hiss
and spit, roil and seethe.

She was old, my mother,
and dead now, or
so they said. Hour after hour
I boiled water
until my walls ran wild
with steam.

Dead

I tell you she was luminous,
my mother, a ballerina
in her blue nightgown
on the undertaker's gray slab
of table. The flaked and wrinkled,
gone. The stroke's wither
and slant, vanished. A man
brought scissors for me to snip
a lock of her silver hair. I reached
to touch one hand. *Where
from here?* I asked. She,
who believed she was sky
to my meadow, was silent.
And I, forever restrained
from showing need, could not fathom
the absence of sun or rain.

Grief

the snowfall all that March,
an aberration this far South,
how it lingered, collaring
the bases of telephone poles,
crusting steps, graying, everywhere
graying, so that riding a bus
(as I seemed to do all that first winter
you were gone) and staring down
into the lumpy graves
of yards, I could no longer imagine
any kind of flowering—not hyacinths
or buttercups, not tulips or larkspur
and surely never again anything
as vibrant as purple bearded iris.

The Young Man in the Obituaries Today

That son, dead from an overdose. Our son,
back in rehab. Why not him?
It could have been him
a dozen times over.

Our garage is full of boxes
from his most recent stay
at a half-way house.
I could go through his clothes, washing, sorting,
folding. Or I could set them all on fire.

The guidebook for those
who love addicts advises:
Neither provoke nor prevent a crisis.

Does it matter?

Now we lay him down to sleep.
Good night, sweet drunk. Sleep
tight 'til hell freezes over.
We want you
gone. We want you
back. Please come back.
Go away. Come back. Stay.

A True Story Longing Wants to Tell

Back when Longing was a reporter
she talked to a twelve-year-old boy who said
finding out he had cancer changed his world
from black and white to Technicolor.

Soon after, Longing got a call
that her son had been in a wreck in a distant town.
Hurry, the doctor breathed into the phone.
On the drive to the hospital, Longing thought
of the young boy whose world had turned bright
with death. Now she watched sun play
the pine needles until they sparkled
like wands, watched each weary bungalow
become an enchanted cottage
where inside a mother was tiptoeing
into her son's room to pull the covers snug to his chin.

III.

I Never Knew I Wanted to Live in a Barn

until I read this line in a poem:
One summer we lived in a barn.
In a flash, I got it: had I spent
one summer in a barn,
I would've known
what the warm oval of an egg
can teach about patience,
how hunger advances
a certain kind of love, erodes
another. How sturdy the fragile
among us, how sometimes unruly
the feathery I might have
learned how dawn can reveal
the edges of delight. How night
tends to stoke the embers of sorrow.
Had I spent one summer in a barn,
I would never have let you go.
I would have known you
in the animal of my bones.

Early Autumn

Fall light played
the room this morning
as if it meant to settle,
its soft roaming smoothing
all the frays. You
might not have noticed,
over there in your chair,
your face deep
in today's news,
but as you read, I watched you
grow younger, plumper, restored
in the beneficent glow.

I lay in bed and waited for you
to look up, hoping
you would see me
as I saw you.
But you read on
and on and too soon,
my love, the old room brightened
and we became again
exactly who we are.

The Landscape of Before

Wind sang through pines. Lopsided moon. Water rushing between
her fingers as if it had lost its way. She loved this island, its feathers
and small, speckled eggs, its ragged edges, tides mimicking
the rhythms of birth. Once the island bore a name, spoken here
and there, inked on ancient maps. Sometimes, in her sleep, she tastes
those days, like something purple and wild that clustered near the shore.

Tourist Season

Such fun we made of the tourists
who clogged our South Florida beaches
every February. Way too early
for the natives to venture into the ocean.
But these women—aging widows,
we supposed, escaping ice and snow—
had scrimped months for this trip
and they were getting wet.

We watched them
wade out—ankles, knees, thighs—
splashing arms, shoulders, necks
until, at last, they were submerged—one
with the dark welter of sea.

In my dream last night, I saw
those long-ago women bobbing
in the ocean, working arms and legs
to keep from going under. One called
my name—though I could barely hear—
and waved for me to swim on out.
I stood on the shore, unable to move
my legs, unable to state my fear.

Photograph

Old woman
holding the golden child
in lamplight
lips parted on a word
we almost feel
lost on air
no longer there
pointing
to a word in the book
lost now or left
somewhere in rain
near the round stones
and the white spirea overgrown
with words
washing away
the old woman
holding the child
in lamplight
spilling still
and gold

This Dream Is a Winter Dream

It sees its breath in the raw air,
watches you wind
through familiar corridors,
as if to a wedding, someone
you have loved for years
waiting. As usual,
you manage to skirt the edge
of pleasure. You turn
from his caress, insist
on the most expensive brand
of champagne. Always something
to singe the gossamer veil.
The trick is to dream
this dream again and again.
Dream it until it rights itself,
until it floats you
through its halls, a silver leaf.

Motel

How dared my parents
make love across the room
in that motel where the child I was
slept on a cot—or where
they thought that child slept—
a starless night somewhere
out West, a thin curtain
of dark between us,
then my father's cigarette,
its roving red tip,
and the match struck just before
that exposed their dear, wicked faces.

The Moviegoer

My father's restless, itching, as usual,
to get out, go somewhere.
Mother's on the sofa, pressing ice
to her migraine. So he pulls me
from my bed—never mind
it's a school night—and soon
we're under stenciled stars at the Tivoli,
watching Grace Kelly in "High Noon."
She's serene and cool beside Gary Cooper
in an open wagon, regal even in black and white.

Take a good look, my father whispers,
pointing up. *Tonight, she's beautiful.*
You'll see. Hollywood will ruin her.

I try to imagine the taste of ruin—
is it something so subtle, so vague,
only he can name it?

I had felt proud that night
to be my father's confidante, to belong
to a man who could predict a starlet's fate
before a prairie shadow ever stained her shoulder.
He must have known things about women
women didn't know about themselves.

Yet something sly and chill
as movie air had slipped in.
My mother at home, in pain, tethered
to a man who could sit beside his daughter
under stars, staking out another woman,
claiming her pure noon as his own.

Longing Finds a Bottle in Her Son's Trash

That bottle's old, he mumbles,
stretching
in the bed. *Let it go.*

Oh, she'd been so proud—
all those months he'd stayed sober,
pulling weeds in her garden,
making the coffee at meetings.

She can't help thinking
of the mortal Niobe,
whose pride in her many offspring
so enraged the gods,
they killed all fourteen
and left their bodies to rot
in the sun. Niobe
they turned into a stone
that still flows with her tears.

Longing hates to admit
her own particular pride—believing
against all reason that her son
had taken his last drink.
She looks down at him now,
still tangled in the sheets,
Niobe's sorrow salting her cheeks.

On Reading that Fourteen Different Feet
Have Washed Up on a Foreign Shore
and Nobody Knows Where They Originated

Imagine your own foot severed,
separated, floating in from who knows
where, wedged into a pile
of logs or trapped alone
in a fishing net. Would you want it
found, ferreted out, exposed?
Better to be lodged somewhere secret
where it can reminisce: the soft
leather of an old ballet slipper
against its toes, the sting
of hot blond sand at its arch. Say
this foot once fell hard for a man
who rubbed it back to life after a day
in a too-snug boot. Say this foot
once danced the Merry Christmas Polka
with an overheated boy and lived
for you to tell the story. This
is the foot, after all, that waded hours
in a cold summer creek, stood patient
beside your mother's grave
as you wept, exposed its sole
as you knelt on the beach to pray
for a lost son. Listen: This foot
has been places—Avila, Cuernavaca,
Tuscany. This foot is not
just any foot. Let it be.

The Father

Is it even possible
my father would have set me up
that way, his younger brother waiting
for us at the Denver airport, the brother
whose infant daughter
had been born
with the cord around her neck.
Is it even possible
my father was coaching me to ask
the unthinkable: *How's the baby?*
I practiced all the way there, knowing
it was wrong, knowing
those words would sting, yet craving
my father's prized wink.
How's the baby? I tried again
under my breath, standing
in the back seat
in my green leggings.
The clouds bulged
with snow. A thin, high wind snaked
through a crack
in the window. I smell it still.

Comfort

I slide my leg
into the still-warm space
in the bed

soaking up
what's left
of your heat

taking it in

the way one takes in
water
after fever

or a cup of tea
at cold dawn

or the way
I sometimes
take you in, deep
into the night of me.

When Her Son Is Six Weeks Sober Longing Drives by His House

She's not checking exactly. Admiring,
is more like it. Fat moon stuck
on a branch of the willow oak, grass
mowed to a sparkle. She slows,
lowers the window, cold air a bright knife
in her throat. She knows he's in there,
sleeping or reading, maybe heating
a pizza. But sober again. *Alive.*
She eases on by, raises the car window,
still smudged, where two months ago,
drunk, begging her for beer money,
he mashed his face to this glass. Lips
like a blowfish. In, out. In, out.

Red Mower, Blue Sky

From where you sit at the table
    playing hearts, you glance across the street
      at the man on the riding mower.

You're unaware you're drinking in
    a profusion of hues and believe
      you're focused only on the game

at hand, or on the cool whirl
    of the ceiling fan. Outside,
      the world is thrown wide

with mad summer, the mower red,
    the man riding it, his white cap,
      the bill pulled low.

With each turn of the machine,
    his body leans out, then back.
      Years later, you will glance up

from your reading
    or your stitching and even
      if it's winter, even if it's dark out

or snowing, you might see the red mower
    still making its way across the lawn,
      the man in the cap

leaning out, blue lacquered
    to the sky, summer green and bright,
      night waiting in the wings.

Morning Lit the Daffodils

In the glass vase on the low table
they appear made of raw silk stitched
and crimped. I call my husband in to look—
Oh, how beautiful! he says—this same husband,
who, when we married forty years ago,
didn't know the name of daffodils
or any other flower and said he didn't care
to know. Since then, so many things
we never predicted—I'll spare you
the list—I only want to say
that every time life surprised,
or thrilled or unleashed,
it did something else as well—eased
into our lives a radiance, yellow on yellow frill.

My Mother-in-Law Sent Sassafras Bark

to help me conceive.
I craved a daughter,
her face like my mother's,
made of sky and leaves
and gentle rain.
I wanted to carry her high
inside, her heft
latching to my heft, her body
a mandolin. Sometimes,
late at night, I hear her
on the stairs or rummaging
through boxes in the attic.
I don't get up. Whatever
she finds she can keep.
Whatever is mine is hers.

She Is Gone

Hours I spend
rummaging around in her Madeline dollhouse,
ivy creeping up the faux brick wall.
I move the grandfather clock to the bedroom.
I fluff the tiny white rug
next to the ivory tub.
As the sun slips behind trees,
I squeeze into her little iron bed.

While Cleaning Out Old Letters to Me from My Husband's Former Girlfriend

I find one in which she uses the phrase,
When at last he was mine. . . referring
to none other than my own. Why
I didn't notice those words
at the time, I can't tell you. When exactly
was he hers? My husband,
of course, swears he can't remember.
When at last he was mine carries
a kind of rough danger,
a ruthless capture, as if she fished him up
from the ocean, arching her back
to reel him in, the line taut,
or lassoed him at a rodeo, hauling him
home dusty and broken, she
in a flannel shirt, sweating
like a cowpoke. At other times,
When at last he was mine
gives me a shivery thrill, conjuring moons
and moors, crashing waves.
Suggesting midnight balconies
and palm-to-palm declarations of love.
When at last he was mine,
When at last he was mine, I've taken
to whispering in my husband's ear.
Rarely have I felt such ardor.

To Minimize How Essential You Are to Me

I sometimes pretend we're in divorce court,
your lips thin and bloodless, your fingers
laced and exact, an axe propped
against your knee. Now I can loathe you
with three bloody chambers of my heart
while, with the fourth, I fall for you
all over again, which reminds me of a story
a friend tells about a friend of hers
whose memory is gone. When this friend
is agitated and nothing will calm her,
the nursing home summons her husband
and somehow, though they've lived apart
a long time, and she has no clue who he is,
he's still the only one who can fold her
into his arms, the only one who can soothe.

Longing Waits in the Narrow Garden

Petals strewn here
and there along the slate path
like careless thoughts.
How she used to sit in this garden, vines
and shrubs nearly obscuring
the outward view, and pretend
she lived somewhere else—a distant town,
perhaps, a place with carousels
with gaily painted horses, gardens
with intricate mazes and lanes
lined with turreted bakeries
that had survived wars and plagues.
This was long ago,
before certain things happened,
before she was able to sit for hours
in the red glider in the garden
at the side of her house and call it paradise.

Poem for an Old Miami Boyfriend

Because I won't be there when he dies,
ask if he remembers
the banyan tree, its roots
braving the air
for something beyond reach.
Ask if he remembers

the thin wash of tide teasing
our feet in the early cove
of morning. The purple streaks
of sky after rain,

gray rooftops glazed with blue.
Ask if he remembers
the texture of flesh
in the warm breath of dark,
all the sad clocks calling us home.

Hold the cup to his lips. Hold his hand.
Because I won't be there
when he dies, ask if he remembers
how true the little worn boat,
its wild bluster.

In the Night, the Wind in the Leaves

swirled and rustled
out our open window as if
for the first time,
as if we never were,
the earth newborn, sweet.

And what of us—asleep
on the too-soft bed
in the old mountain house?

Gone.

Also our children.
The ones who lived, the ones who died
before they grew whole. All night

the breeze swirled and rustled
through the leaves as if it played
a secret game, swirling
and rustling all night

as if we never were.

NOTES

I am indebted to Jaime Zuckerman whose poem, "Becoming," included the line that inspired my poem, "I Never Knew I Wanted to Live in a Barn."

I am also indebted to the late Donald Justice, whose poem "Psalm and Lament" begins with the line, "The clocks are sorry, the clocks are very sad," which inspired my line about "all the sad clocks calling us home," in the poem, "Poem for an Old Miami Boyfriend."

I am grateful to the Hackney Literary Award for honoring "Secret" with First Prize in its 2018 nationwide contest.

Cover artist Dawn Surratt studied art at the University of North Carolina at Greensboro as a recipient of the Spencer Love Scholarship in Fine Art. She has exhibited her work throughout the Southeast and currently works as a freelance designer and artist. Her work has been published internationally in magazines, on book covers, and in print media. She lives on the beautiful Kerr Lake in northern North Carolina with her husband, one demanding cat, and a crazy Pembroke Welsh Corgi.

Dannye Romine Powell is the author of four previous collections, two of which have won the Brockman-Campbell Award for the best book of poetry published by a North Carolinian in the previous year. She's won fellowships in poetry from the NEA, the North Carolina Arts Council and the writer's colony Yaddo. Her poems have appeared in many magazines and journals, among them *The Paris Review*, *Ploughshares*, *32 Poems*, *Harvard Review Online*, *The Southern Review*, *The Beloit Poetry Journal*, *Cave Wall* and *Tar River*. A long-time book editor for the *Charlotte Observer*, Powell is also the author of *Parting the Curtains: Interviews with Southern Writers*. She lives in a yellow house across from a park with her husband Lew Powell, also a long-time journalist.

CPSIA information can be obtained
at www.ICGtesting.com
Printed in the USA
BVHW030034070520
578330BV00001B/1

9 781950 413225